CHIANG MAI

THAILAND TRAVEL GUIDE

EAT, SLEEP AND PARTY YOUR WAY ACROSS

CHIANG MAI

W. Johnson

Copyright 2016 - All Rights Reserved – *W. Johnson*

ALL RIGHTS RESERVED. No part of this publication may be reproduced or transmitted in any form whatsoever, electronic, or mechanical, including photocopying, recording, or by any informational storage or retrieval system without express written, dated and signed permission from the author.

TABLE OF CONTENTS

Introduction — 5
Getting to know Chiang Mai — 7
History of Chiang Mai — 9
Weather and Climate — 12
Getting to Chiang Mai — 13
    Flying — 13
    Bus and Train — 15
Getting around Chiang Mai — 16
    Bus — 16
    Taxis — 16
    Tuk-tuk — 17
    Songthaew — 17
Seeing Chiang Mai — 19
    Historical Chiang Mai — 19
    Natural Chiang Mai — 27
    Cultural Chiang Mai — 32
Festivals — 43
Nightlife — 46
Accommodation — 49
    Budget Accommodation — 50

Mid Range Accommodation	51
High End Accommodation	51
Eating Out	**53**
Conclusion	**56**

INTRODUCTION

When many people plan trips to Thailand they are often thinking about magnificent white beaches sheltered by cliffs, swimming in water so blue it will make you thirsty just thinking about it, dream islands where the inhabitants do nothing but party, or the neon buzz of Bangkok clouded with the steam of street side noodles.

What many don't expect is the chilled-out and fascinating cultural center that is the city of Chiang Mai.

A city that is rich in Buddhist tradition and inhabited by monks, craftspeople and artists from all over the world. A city where ancient Thailand, with its 700-year-old city walls and temples, meets all the modern delights the country has to offer with some of the best food and entertainment in South East Asia.

You can wake up in the morning to visit a 3D art gallery or take a cooking class and then spend the evening exploring rainforest and rice paddies on the back of an elephant.

Of all of the tourist attractions in Thailand, Chiang Mai is the one held dearest by many locals and with good reason. It offers tranquility, beauty, and fun in equal measure. Luckily these locals know how to enjoy themselves and can help you discover Chiang Mai without getting stung like a tourist.

To discover all the religious monuments, historical sites, delicious eateries, exciting festivals and parties, and the surrounding hillside wildlife you will need help: which is where this guide comes in.

After a brief rundown of the history of Chiang Mai you will be given guidance on the best way to get in and out, what you need to see and what you don't, the latest and greatest restaurants and hotels to check out, and how to get the most out of your stay in this magical part of Thailand.

Welcome to Chiang Mai.

GETTING TO KNOW CHIANG MAI

Chiang Mai is both a city and the epicenter of the Chiang Mai province – one of Thailand's 76 provinces. It is the second largest province in the country with over one million inhabitants (with 200,000 living directly in the city and 400,000 in its wider area) and is the heartland of Northern Thailand.

Over 70% of this province is forest or countryside which leaves you plenty of room to go trekking or boating, and being in the shadow of Doi Inthanon and Doi Chiang Dao, the two largest mountains in Thailand, there is no reason you wouldn't want to.

Thanks to this greenery, until the 1920s getting to Chiang Mai required an elephant-fueled expedition just to reach it. Getting there now is a simple train ride, but this delay in development does mean that Chiang Mai is one of the last big cities in Thailand to still truly capture the feeling of old Thailand.

A feeling that is no better encapsulated than by its old city: a neat square surrounded by a moat and walled off to the bustle of the rest of the city that is growing out and up (building height is severely restricted in the old city).

Of the 300 or so temples to be found in the city the most magnificent are located here in walking distance of each other; including Wat Chiang Man and Wat Phra Singh. Come on weekends to find authentic markets selling a whole manner of wares you won't be able to fit in your luggage home.

Outside the old city is the new city, or new town centre, which is home to restaurants, museums, markets, and shops galore. The arguable main thoroughfare for many is Nimmanhaemn Road: the hip district populated by locals and students where you will find the biggest clubs and trendiest restaurants (though decidedly fewer temples than the rest of the city).

To the east of the old city is the Ping River, which is where a lot of the new city is centered and many pretty riverside restaurants are located.

Go a little further out, about 9 miles to be exact, and you start inclining upwards to Doi Suthep: a modest mountain, which at 6,000 feet, towers over the city and is home to the breath-taking Wat Phrathat Doi Suthep. Not for those afraid of stairs but not to be missed either.

HISTORY OF CHIANG MAI

The history of Chiang Mai does not begin as a history of Thailand but as one of the Lanna Kingdom.

The Lawa people have long lived in this part of Northern Thailand and many still continue to live in the mountains around the areas (numbering as many as 17,000), where they continue to live traditional lifestyles and many still speak Lua instead of Thai.

Prior to 1296 and the founding of Chiang Mai, another city called Wiang Nopburi was the hub of the Ling Valley and the Lawa people. Thanks to its struggles with flooding it had a troubled history and its ruins are a popular tourist attraction today.

Chiang Mai, as the city we know it as, was founded in 1296 by King Mangrai of the Lanna Kingdom with the intention of being its new capital. The city was surrounded by a wall and moat to guard it against the threat of the Burmese and Mongolian empires.

The Lanna Kingdom had mixed fortunes for most of its existence until instability in its royal family allowed its walled city fall to the powers of the Burmese Empire in 1558. After a series of struggles with independence, the Burmese empire used Chiang Mai as a base to invade and conquer Siam (the former name of Thailand) and China in the 1760s.

The Burmese grip on the region was, however, quite weak and by 1775 the Lanna Kingdom became the Kingdom of Chiang Mai and an outlier state of Siam. During this time Burma continued to try and re-take their old haunt with such ferocity that Chiang Mai was abandoned for over 10 years between 1776 and 1791.

It was around this time in the early 1800s, that the large brick wall was built around the city and it was established as a river port.

In the late 1880s, the British Empire had taken over Burma which led to them discovering Chiang Mai and its surrounding mountains and woodlands. British interests grew in the area which began to cause issues for Bangkok ruled Siam. It became necessary for Siam to increase its hold on the Chiang Mai area and by the early 1900s Chiang Mai was largely a province of Siam, though not officially one until 1933. Siam itself officially became Thailand in 1939.

It was in 1921 that Chiang Mai opened itself up with its railway and by 1960s tourism became the city's main trade, but its production of craft items and pottery still remains an important part of its economy. Chiang Mai has grown to arguably become Thailand's second city, and now has a growing ex-pat community with many residents coming from all around the world.

WEATHER AND CLIMATE

Being in the mountains and higher up than a lot of Thailand, Chiang Mai is markedly cooler than its southern counterpart. A fact not overlooked by locals who often come here for respite in the summer months.

It has a wet and dry tropical climate with fairly consistent warmth year round. Though, keep in mind that things can get quite chilly at night during the dry seasons (between December and March).

Temperatures rest in the high 20s in Celsius and the high to low 90s in Fahrenheit throughout much of the year, with a bit more heat during typical summer months.

Expect a considerable amount of rain in the wet season, especially in August and September where 7/10 days will have rain with as much as 8.5 inches coming down (double what you'd get in a place like New York City at it wettest). Clouds can act as a natural shelter but it will be very humid.

In the dry season you will see almost no rain. So pack your clothes accordingly. More recently the city has some issues with air pollution so be prepared if this has been an issue for you in other big cities.

GETTING TO CHIANG MAI

Thailand is quite a long and thin country with its famous beaches in the south near Phuket, its luscious mountains in the north in Chiang Mai and Bangkok somewhere in the middle of this straight line.

For most people that will fly straight into Bangkok it will be a matter of choosing whether they go north or south first, before going the other way and then finishing up in Bangkok before they leave.

With flights from the rest of Europe and America to Bangkok being sometimes half the price of a flight to Chiang Mai, and with trains and domestic flights being so cheap this is often the most cost effective way to approach Thailand and Chiang Mai. Flying into Phuket or Chiang Mai first might be best in terms of logistics, but you will still need to change at Bangkok and of course if you fly into Phuket first and fly out of Chiang Mai, you will be paying twice as much on both flights.

FLYING

Assuming you are coming to Chiang Mai from Bangkok, you have a few different options. Flying is easy and there are nearly hourly flights between the two cities and the flight itself will take an average of one hour and ten minutes.

One-way with taxis will cost you about 1,500 baht or $40, but if you book in advance in the cheaper months (and use a comparison website like Skyscanner) you can do the trip one-way for as little as $20 on specific days (flight is $10 and getting to and from the airport is $10). For comparison it could cost you as much as $150 more to fly directly to Chiang Mai as it would to Bangkok from many locations.

The airport is only 2 miles from the city but will cost you at least 50 baht by bus and about 150 baht if you take a taxi (you can see if fellow travelers will split the fare with you).

BUS AND TRAIN

A bus direct to Chiang Mai is available from Bangkok and will take between 9 and 12 hours depending on whether you go for express or not and will cost between 400 and 800 baht ($11 and $22). You will either get to Arcade Bus Station or Chang Phuak Bus Station and it will cost you as much as 100 baht to get to the center of the city (to and from bus stations or airports is always going to cost you more, if you are feeling sprightly you might want to walk a bit closer before getting a taxi or songthaew).

A train will take you about 15 hours and there are regular journeys, prices will range from 120 to 300 baht depending on the class you get (third class does not come with air conditioning). Overnight sleeper trains cost up to 1400 baht.

The cheaper buses are not always the most comfortable and if you get on a dud it can be a very long and smelly journey. In general, though the quality is quite good and the express service has reasonable time and conditions. Thai trains are usually kept to an excellent standard with good clean facilities and even a disco at night in the dining cart. Make sure whatever you do to book in advance and to keep in mind that air conditioning can get very cold.

By land the journeys can be pretty to look at, but if you have time to book your tickets in advance (especially in the rainy season) then flying will give you an extra day in Chiang Mai for the same price and you won't get stuck next to a smelly bus toilet for an entire day.

Chiang Mai is a very interesting city and region in general, so how long you spend is really up to you. Many people find they love the chilled-out environment and stay longer than the basic three or four days most people have in mind.

GETTING AROUND CHIANG MAI

Chiang Mai is not the largest city in the world and much of the interesting sites are quite close together in the center. With enough time and some good planning, you will be able to quite happily walk between several destinations with fewer headaches than haggling for several rides a day might ensue.

It can, however, get hot and the sidewalk isn't always the most complimentary surface to your feet in Chiang Mai.

BUS

Buses are comfortable and relatively easy to use to get between the bigger sites and views in the city. If you want to go to more specific locations you may find yourself getting dazed with the giant network and the language barrier, but it should never be too difficult to get to the bigger tourist sites.

The B1 and B2 bus will hit most of the big destinations in the city and will cost you at least 15 baht ($0.50).

TAXIS

Taxis need to be booked over the phone or you can pick them at big spots such as train stations or bigger hotels. They are not typically available to be flagged down on the street otherwise.

Usually there is a 150 baht minimum for locations around the centre and a higher fee once you try to get out of the city. This is mainly an option for larger groups but it can be an easy and relatively good value way of getting around.

TUK-TUK

Tuk-tuks and smaller, and slower, three-wheel bicycles known as samlor are found all around the city. They can be decent value for smaller trips at 50 baht for a short trip and between 100 to 150 baht for longer trips. They will often not go too far outside of really popular destinations without charging you a lot for it.

You should try tuk-tuk at least once if you haven't before, but they are not always the most efficient or quietest route.

SONGTHAEW

One of the more unique pieces of transport in Chiang Mai is the songthaew: a truck with several benches in the back. You will find some are on a fixed route and others can be chartered by you to get around or out of the city. Songthaew can be excellent value if you are travelling with several different people.

Fixed journeys will cost you 20 baht and having a personal journey can cost anywhere from 20 to 200 baht. You will need to haggle and make sure you are paying per person (you might find the pretty cheap price you got turns out to be per person if you don't specify while haggling).

This is how many locals choose to travel and they have their favorite routes that they know work well. With transport though, you may find that being more like a local is less desirable as getting around the old city is different than getting around the suburbs and you don't want to waste too much time getting around cheaply, if it means seeing the backseat of a car or bus instead of Chiang Mai.

SEEING CHIANG MAI

Chiang Mai and its surrounding areas have a lot to offer and it will be very much up to you to cater your stay to your interests: and Chiang Mai is a city that caters to nearly all of them.

This guide will split points of interest in Chiang Mai between Historical, Natural and Cultural. Most travelers will find they want to experience all three and some of the best temples and historical sites, most notably Doi Suthep, will require a bit of trekking to see anyway.

Chiang Mai does not have the same whirlwind party lifestyle of Phuket or Bangkok or their streets of unbridled adult entertainment, but it has more than enough of its own characteristic relaxing nights of pleasure, partying and entertainment to offer to keep even the most excitable traveler happy.

HISTORICAL CHIANG MAI

If you've come all the way to Chiang Mai then at some point you have to visit some its magnificent temples. They might be tourist bait, but it is delicious bait nonetheless and some of it cannot be ignored. Plus, entry to many of the temples is free or very cheap.

With over 300 temples in the area you will need guidance on which you need to see and which you could wait to see on a longer stay.

Not surprisingly for a region that has changed hands to several different rulers and empires over the years, its temples and churches have a wider variety of architectural trademarks behind them than some temples in the south, but the principle religion here is Theravada Buddhism and most of the grander temples abide by this tradition.

Only a few of the more impressive temples will require you to go out of your way to see them, and many others can be happily folded into your travels and treks around the region (30 of them are in the old city). Similarly, the walls of Chiang Mai's old city demand to be explored but you can explore them at your leisure as you see the rest of the city.

Remember that you must dress respectfully at all temples in Thailand, which means taking your shoes off before entering a temple and making sure you are dressed modestly (no naked shoulders or cleavage) and most of your legs will need to be covered from above the ankle.

If you think you are going to get too hot, consider taking something you can wrap around you or trousers that break down into shorts. It's only in the temples you need to dress modestly. Don't worry too much about the safety of your shoes: locals respect the temples and don't steal from them. If anyone suggests a fee for looking after your shoes ignore them.

Must See Temples

Without trying to be dismissive of Chiang Mai's many temples there are a few that will raise eyebrows if you don't visit, and they will be eyebrows raised for good reason.

Wat Phrathat Doi Suthep

Wat Phrathat is one temple you can't avoid seeing in Chiang Mai because it towers over it around the slopes of Doi Suthep.

The story behind the temple is that in 1383 a piece of shoulder bone belonging to Buddha was sent to Chiang Mai. On its journey to Chiang Mai the bone broke in two, one half is kept at Wat Suan Dok and the other was given to a white elephant that was left to wander the jungle and Doi Suthep until its trumpeted loudly three times and died. The location of the elephant's last days was used as the site for Way Phrathat.

Getting to the starting point of the famed steps of Wat Phrathat can be tricky. There are many ways to save money and get there and back for 100 baht or less but most songthaew taxi's will take you there for 200 baht from the old city of Chiang Mai, which will take approximately 40 minutes.

Chiang Mai Travel Guide

With a bit more haggling and discussion you can get the Songthaew to cart you around for half a day for about 400 baht, and you will get to see some impressive gardens and a hillside village known as Khun Chankian Homg Village: a must if you want to see an authentic rural Thai village.

Getting to and from Chiang Mai Zoo is cheaper than the temple (and not so far away) so you might want to break up your trip by stopping there first or on your way back.

There is a lot to see around the temple so leave plenty of time. The big question once you get there is whether you want to walk the stairs or not. There are 300 of them up steep mountainside or a cable car with no view for 20 baht. Try to walk if you can and perhaps consider taking the cable car down if you aren't feeling too up to it on the way back. Entrance will cost 30 baht if you are not a local.

Wat Chiang Man

Wat Chiang Man is the oldest temple in the city, being built in 1296. It's within easy access to most destinations being in the old city. It's open until 6 and entry is free (though you may feel the need for giving a donation which will be warmly received).

It is a fascinating temple with Sri Lankan architecture around it and is home to what are claimed to be two of the oldest images of Buddha in the world with the oldest clocking in at 2,500 years old.

Wat Chedi Luang

Wat Chedi Luang is one of the biggest temples in the city and was the largest building in the city for a long time after being built in 1441 until an earthquake took it down a few pegs. Again this is free and open until 6 pm.

It's a fascinating temple with a more wayward and ruinous vibe than some of its scrubbed up counterparts. Definitely worth a visit to see what Lanna-style temples would have been like and what old Chiang Mai looked like.

Wat Phra Singh

Wat Phra Singh is the most famous temple in Chiang Mai and Thai people come from all over the country just to look upon the famous image of Buddha contained within its walls of a chapel behind the main temple.

It is a classic looking Thai temple and makes great use of the regions beloved teak wood. It is open until later at 8.30 pm, but it also has a 20 baht entry free: worth paying to see the temple at least once.

Wat Umong

Wat Umong is a little out of the way of the old city, and much less noisy and crammed than its famed friends listed above. What makes this such a fascinating temple is that large parts of it are built underground and it is known as a cave temple.

If you are going to see a lot of temples in Thailand, make this one of them as it is quite unique. The temple is near Chiang Mai University and you'll need to make sure you are heading to the right temple if you are getting a ride. Entry is free and it is open until 6pm.

Phu Ping Palace

You can see this palace and its marvelous gardens near Doi Suthep, this can be overlooked by tourists because it's not dripping with religion and history, but it is a well-kept and beautiful authentic Thai garden to relax in for a while. Entry is 50 baht and it is open until 3pm.

The Old City

You will most likely stay near or around the old city so you don't need to be told to visit it, but do take the time to walk around its walls, moats and awe-inspiring gates while you are here.

NATURAL CHIANG MAI

Chiang Mai is surrounded by mountains, rivers, and jungle and locals and foreigners alike come here for serene treks through the beautiful city and countryside.

Whether you are on the back of a bike or an elephant or just plodding along on your own two feet there is a lot to see here in Chiang Mai, and there is something to meet the desires of every type of adventurer.

Mountains

Doi Inthanon National Park

Doi Inthanon or the roof of Thailand is the highest mountain in the country at 8415 feet high. At that height, you are unlikely to choose to climb to the top without a previous desire to do so, but the mountain is inside a national park about 40 miles outside of Chiang Mai and that is worth a visit.

It will likely cost you 2000 baht to get here by songthaew and has a 300 baht entry fee. You can opt to rent a car or motorbike for the day if you prefer. There are a lot of trails to spend your day on here as well as the Borichinda Cave, the Thai National Observatory, a couple of temples and some picturesque waterfalls, including Mae Klang Waterfall.

Home to cloud forest, bogs, and deciduous forest there is a lot of interesting nature and wildlife to see here. Being slightly cooler, many locals travel out here to escape the heat or crowds if they feel the need.

Pha Daeng National Park

This is the home of Chiang Dao, a limestone mountain towering at 7174 feet high and surrounded by beautiful trails and wildlife. It is 40 miles north of Chiang Mai, you can get a bus headed to Thaton and it will cost about 40 baht.

There is a lot to see around here including trails, waterfalls, an unlit 8-mile-long cave, hot springs, a campsite, and every Tuesday there is a market that sells fantastic local wears. Not as well known as Inthanon, but worth a day if you are an outdoorsman and intend to be staying around Chiang Mai for a long time.

Elephants

Seeing Thailand on the back of an Elephant is something that is seen by many tourists as a must, and for a long time was the traditional method of travel for kings and nobles. You do need to be careful when choosing to see or ride an elephant, as the treatment of elephants in some parts of Thailand is not ideal and you don't want to put elephants under stress for a novelty ride.

There are many places to go and see elephants where you can be sure they are treated well. There is far more to do here than just ride elephants, however. At some sanctuaries you can bathe alongside elephants or even play with them if that is your choice.

If you are in doubt, check to see if the place is accredited by a trusted wildlife organization: there are more than enough reasonably priced ones that you won't have to settle for one that isn't.

Elephant Nature Park

Elephant Nature Park is probably the most popular park for visiting elephants in Chiang Mai: it is a home for rescued elephants and the main idea is to help you discover these animals in a respectful way. You will get to interact, bathe and even play with elephants but you won't see them performing for you.

You can visit for the day including transport for 2,500 baht a day.

Eddy Elephant Care Chiang Mai

Eddy's elephants are a great way to get in to close contact with an elephant and to act as an elephant owner for the day. You'll see how best to look after them, how to train one, how to clean one and how to have fun with one. You will also get a ride through the jungle. (Comes with lunch and transport from Chiang Mai for 2,300 a day)

Chiang Mai Night Safari

Chiang Mai's night safari has gotten very popular recently, so it's worth mentioning here. It's really just a tour of the Chiang Mai zoo at night complete with a bit of show around.

If you really want to see a zoo and get close to some of the animals it's not a bad option, but it's not exactly essential if you don't have a desire to feed animals at night. It costs 100 baht for walking and 800 baht for a guided tour but many guests complain of a poor service.

Hillside Tribe Tour

Visiting one of the several authentic hillside tribes around Chiang Mai is a must if you are staying here for a few days, and you have never been to one before in Southeast Asia. You will get to see thatched roof villages surrounding eye-watering green jungle.

The best way to do this is with a guided tour if you're not too confident on your own on Thai roads. It is important you pick an ethical tour that respects the village and is not going to try and con you into buying Chinese-made souvenirs. When you do visit be respectful of the locals and their ways, and avoid giving gifts directly to children if you feel inclined to, and instead ask your guide who best to give things to.

Baan Tong Luang is a government sponsored Hill Tribe that is there to show tourists what a village should look like, without disturbing locals.

You will want to be careful of avoiding the tourist heavy villages closest to Chiang Mai, but if you don't have much time you may have to settle for something closer. There is nothing wrong with these places, but you may feel awkward with large throngs of people snapping pictures of real people in their daily life.

Thailand Hilltribe Holidays does a good job of providing interesting and ethical trips around authentic villages. Prices will vary a lot and you could opt to rent a bike and visit some yourself.

Raft Tours

Rafting is something that is done mostly by locals as it is not exactly the main idea many foreigners have in mind when they come to see jungles and elephants. Going down the Mae Tang River can be an interesting way to see the area and there are a few rapids to keep the whole thing exciting.

There are several tour companies that will offer trips at reasonable prices so don't be afraid to look them up. You can also opt for a cruise of Mae Ping River which is a pleasant trip and costs 450 baht.

Canopy Tour

For a fee of 3600 baht you can have an adventure tour of the rainforest around Chiang Mai, which is quite a thrilling experience since the Flight of the Gibbon Tour Company has 3 miles of zip lines and lots of fun add-ons throughout.

Not an essential part of the trip and at $100 you could probably have as much fun on a zip line tour back home, but this may be the only time you can do it in a Thai jungle. Set aside most of the day if you choose to do this.

CULTURAL CHIANG MAI

Modern Chiang Mai has more than enough to offer visitors away from the jungles and several-hundred-year-old temples. Later there will be an entire chapter on Northern Thai food and getting your fill of it in Chiang Mai, so this chapter is going to cover things to do in Chiang Mai for the discerning tourist.

Markets

Markets are not just hangouts for quirky middle class people on weekends in Chiang Mai: they are an important part of daily life and really give a feel of electricity and character of the city. You won't have a much better opportunity than getting lost in one of the city's bazaars.

Warorot

Warorot is the oldest market still running in Chiang Mai and it is enormous. Its heart is inside a several-story shopping centre selling clothes, food, trinkets, toys and more. It then spreads out for several streets selling goods in the open air.

It closes at about 6pm for the inside market and 11pm for the outside. It is east of the old city and close to the Ping River. A lot of the fresh food, antiques and clothes may be impractical for you to buy, but soaking up the atmosphere is worth an afternoon. Keep in mind that Thai clothes may not be built with Western frames and body shapes in mind, so be careful when you buy anything.

This is also the location of Chiang Mai's Chinatown which is worth a visit just for its vibrancy.

Weekend Night Market

On Saturday and Sunday night you will find markets on Wualai Road and Rachadamnonen Road, respectively. You will need to turn up after around 5pm when things get started and you can find a huge range of craft items, tourist tat, and other figurines, toys, antiques and plenty of snacks and treats on offer. Expect crowds at busy times of the year.

Night Bazaar

The Night Bazaar is the main haggle spot for tourists, and as such you can expect to find oodles of gifts and souvenirs at probably the best prices in the city if you are persistent enough.

It starts after 7pm every night of the week, and is located east of the old city's Phae Gate. Worth a visit if you are in the area and you have had your share of temples for the day. There is also some excellent food and fashion on offer here so come hungry. It can get busy and things tend to get crowded so feel free to come later so long as you are there by midnight.

Kham Tiang and Ton Lam Yai are the city's two biggest flower markets and are worth a visit if you happen to be in the areas around them.

Museums

There are several museums in Chiang Mai and while some of them are the usual tourist traps, a few are definitely worth fitting into your itinerary and some, like the Art In Paradise Gallery (with their 3D paintings) near the Night Bazaar, are worth visiting if you have children with you or you get caught in the rain.

Lanna Folklife Museum

This is an interesting little museum about the history of the Lanna kingdom. They have some good explanations of what you are looking at, and a decent collection.

Not essential but it's good for context and it is easy to get to from the Three King's Monument in the old city. Open until 5pm and it costs 90 baht for an adult to get in.

Chiang Mai City Arts and Cultural Centre

Despite the potentially dry name, this isn't just a venue for local shows and artists but a large and well maintained exhibit that is worth seeing to view artifacts of old Chiang Mai and its turbulent history.

The building is an interesting throwback to the colonial architecture of days gone by, and you should make an effort to stop here for a quick tour if you are blank about Chiang Mai's history. Found in the centre of the old city, it's open until 5pm and costs 90 baht per adult.

Chiang Mai Tribal Museum

If you are interested in the slower and traditional aspects of Thai life that its cities haven't given you then the tribal visit is definitely worth a visit. It is quite an open museum, so you are not just confined to a few small rooms and there is quite a lot to take in.

It is in the north of the city on Chang Puak Road, it is open between 8am and 4pm (with an hour lunch break) and it costs 50 baht for an adult. It's a relatively quiet museum so you can take your time and relax here.

Cookery Classes

Cooking classes in Chiang Mai can be quite invigorating. These are some two hour demonstrations with an entire afternoon of hands on experience, usually starting with a trip to the market where you will be shown where to get the best produce.

If you are at all interested in Thai cooking, some of these classes are really fantastic experiences that will let you take home more than a plastic Buddha. Remember to book in advance and to set aside enough time to get it all done.

Red Chili Cooking School

This class lasts from 8am to 3pm and comes with transport and of course food. You will learn a lot here from an experienced Thai chef who gives fantastic lessons in an authentic setting.

Aroy Aroy Thai Cooking School

This cooking class is located near a Rivery Market Restaurant and you will get a boat trip around the market for fresh food and then back to prepare one of a variety of different menus. Expect small class sizes and excellent teachers.

Pantawan Cooking School

Comes with a trip to the market and is a slightly fancy affair, with the class being taught in a traditional teak home. Classes are based on themes centered on traditional Thai cuisine. You are even given a certificate at the end.

Spas and massage

Massages are a different phenomenon in Thailand than in the West. They're not seen as exclusive luxury pampering sessions, or slightly sleazy affairs that must come with a happy ending.

Instead they are seen as nourishing and often spiritual activities, and as such they are cheap and plentiful. Chiang Mai is an especially good Thai city if you are interested in getting good quality massages, and especially getting traditional Thai massages. Relaxation is something Chiang Mai is quickly developing a monopoly on, and there are luxury hotel spas, wellness centers and boutique parlors everywhere you go.

One of the best experiences is getting a massage at a temple. Many of them have them on offer as they are seen as important methods of healing the mind and body. Wat Mahawan is located a short walk east of Tha Phae Gate of the old city, and is well-known for its excellent massages. At 140 baht for a traditional Thai massage, it's worth finding out if it lives up to its reputation.

If you are looking for a more traditional parlour or spa you might want to try:

Vian Ping Massage and Spa

Vian Ping is located just a little east of Wat Mahawan outside of the old city. It is a little more organized and high-class than some of its counterparts and you will get an excellent Thai massage here or you can opt for one of their many other relaxing treatments.

It costs between 200 and 250 baht for a massage. You'll struggle to find better inside Thailand for this price.

Green Bamboo Massage

Green Bamboo is a favorite among tourist and locals, alike. Many come for its traditional Chiang Mai teak architecture, and many more come because the staff is incredibly friendly and experienced. Tea and snacks are provided while you are massaged. Prices start at 200 baht, but they are more than worth it.

Chiang Mai Women's Prison Massage Centre (or correctional institute)

One Thai initiative to get female felons back on track is to get them next to the massage table, and with this massage centre being one of the most popular in Chiang Mai it must be doing something right.

It is located helpfully near the Three King's Monument in the old city, and you can get a full body massage at the slightly lower price of 180 baht. This is a completely different experience from anywhere else, and since most travelers will be able to afford several massages when they are in Chiang Mai, this should be on your itinerary if you are in the market for relaxation.

San Kamphaeng Hot Springs

Chiang Mai is a mountainous region and it comes with its own hot spring retreat you can try out if you have a long stay in the city. Reports say that tourists (or farangs as they are often called in Thailand) will be charged 100 baht to get entry for the day, but it advertises its prices as 40 baht for entry.

The springs are located thirty miles outside the city and it will cost you possibly up to 200 baht to get there by public transport. It's not the most popular attraction and as far as hot springs go it's not that special unless you buy some of the more spurious claims that sulfur has magical healing properties.

Why mention it then? Simply because it offers the great Thai tradition of having boiled eggs while you soak. Eggs are available to buy at the counter so you can boil them yourself in some of the hotter springs.

Muay Thai

Thai boxing, or Muay Thai, is a fascinating blend of boxing, kick boxing and martial arts. It is an interesting spectacle to see and gives you a real taste of authentic Chiang Mai culture. You can even take part in the frenzied betting, if you want to indulge in the Asian gambling stereotype.

There are different venues all around the city. Kalare and Tha Phae stadium are nearest the old city and you can spend an evening watching several hours of men fighting each other in the ring for between 400 to 600 baht.

Muay Thai is immensely popular in Thailand and if you are here long enough and the idea doesn't put you off, it is an essential Thai experience.

Bootcamp Fitness

Bootcamp can be a very effective way to lose weight and get in shape very fast. Gym Bangarang is located in Mae Rim about thirty minutes from Chiang Mai. This gym offers muay thai, CrossFit, boxing, rock climbing, personalized weight loss programs, meal plans, weight lifting, and more. Gym Bangarang is a one of kind holiday fitness destination for athletes.

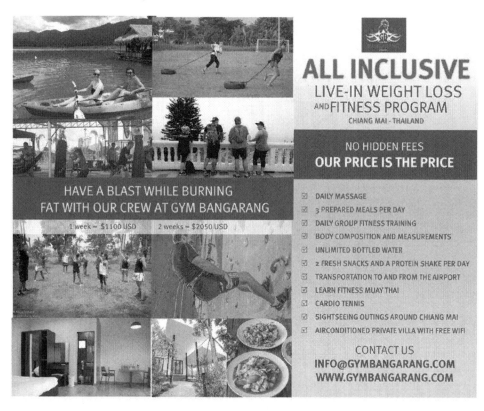

FESTIVALS

Chiang Mai is home to several festivals throughout the year, and it is the best place to come if you want to see these celebrations in their truest traditional forms. Many of the bigger festivals are family oriented events, lasting several days underpinned with Buddhist rituals.

Keep in mind that several of the festivals are big deals and the city becomes quite busy when they are on. If you are not interested, then consider waiting until it is over so you can see the city in relative peace. The dates of festivals can vary from year to year so make sure you are up-to-date when booking anything as you don't want to miss out by a day or two.

Songkran Festival

Songkran is a unique water festival that is celebrated across Thailand and there are similar festivals in surrounding Southeast Asian countries. The basic idea is to celebrate the traditional new year for three days between the 13th and 15th of April with an enormous water fight.

Chiang Mai is particularly famed for its celebrations and there will be much drunken revelry and people being drenched by strangers with buckets of water over their head. You probably don't need to be told to dress appropriately.

Among all the water-based fun there is a more spiritual and serious side to the celebrations with monk-led ceremonies and parades being held around Tha Pae Gate, and the wider city towards the Ping River.

Bo Sang Umbrella Festival

It probably sounds like this festival should be combined with Songkran, but there is much less water fighting at the umbrella festival. It is held yearly around mid January. It is held in the village of Bo Sang which is only a short trip to the outskirts of the city.

The main draw is the huge range of handmade umbrellas and other hand crafted wares on offer. There are also a huge range of games, entertainment and traditional rituals and cultural displays. You can even see the new Miss Bo Sang being crowned.

Yi Peng and Loy Krathong

There are two festivals held at the same time in Chiang Mai thanks to its varied history. The first is Yin Peng which is celebrated across Thailand on the full moon of the 2nd month of what is known as the Lanna calendar (which is roughly around November).

There are many traditions behind the Yi Peng festival but it could best be called the lantern festival. During the celebration millions of lanterns are lit and sent into the skies and houses are decorated with ornate paper lanterns.

Loy Krathong is held on the full moon as well, but it is held on the 12th month of the Thai Lunar calendar (which is the same full moon as the one above). The celebration is quite fascinating and thousands of people come out to float figurines shaped like lotuses (made out of various goodies and banana trunk) down various streams and rivers. In addition, many choose to float candles down the river, which makes for a truly magical night.

Flower Festival

Chiang Mai's flower festival is a really beautiful occasion held over three days in early February. The entire city is festooned with different flowers and flower decorations which culminate together at the Suan Buak Haad in the southern part of the old city.

Gardeners compete for the best trees and flowers, carnivals are held, vibrant parades course through the city's streets, and there is a much loved beauty contest as well.

NIGHTLIFE

It has long been the rule that you go to Bangkok to party and come to Chiang Mai to relax, but just because things are more relaxed doesn't mean people don't know how to have a good time.

The chilled-out vibe of the city comes through in its nightlife as well with more than enough excellent (and sometimes cheesy) live music and events to fill up on. Much of which is far less intense and more wholesome than you might find elsewhere.

If you do want to party hard though, Chiang Mai has plenty to offer in the way of parties, bars, and nightclubs. You'll find here as well, that you are partying alongside locals and Thai students instead of thousands of sweaty farangs, and the touts looking to rip them off.

If you are looking for the more chilled out and casual nights out, you will want to head east of the old city towards the Night Bazaar and the riverside. There are many bars and venues along the river if you are looking for a quiet (or not so quiet drink), at a reasonable price.

If you are looking for live music you might want to try the Boy Blues Bar, Chiang Mai Riverside Restaurant, Kat Bar, or the North Gate Jazz Co-Op. For slightly raunchier or livelier entertainment you may want to head over to the Chiang Mai Entertainment Complex at the Night Bazaar.

Here you can find nightclubs, Muay Thai fights, go-go dancers, and more. If you want to branch out a little, then try the Fabrique Nightclub and Bubbles Nightclub which are not far away. You will find everything from tourist hotspots, to expat hang outs, to local favorites around here.

If you want to have a really good trip with the hippest party-goers, the consensus is out and you need to head west from the old city to Nimmanhaeman. It's not the most glamorous location, but thanks to its proximity to Chiang Mai's main university you will always find that it is alive.

If you want to see live music the Bridge Bar is the main venue around here. The clubs and restaurants have a distinctly up-market and quirky vibe to them so you can pick whichever interests you. Monkey Club and Warm Up Bar are the two most popular clubs in the city with its young locals: if that is who you want to be around then get here when things heat up after 10pm.

ACCOMMODATION

Chiang Mai is really an excellent value for places to stay and sleep: even by Thai standards.

If you are looking for super budget accommodations, you can stay in one of the many hostels for as little as 100 baht a night for a dorm bed. For only a little more though, at between 200 and 500 baht, you can get your own room in a guesthouse or small hotel.

If you go too cheap you are not always guaranteed air conditioning or even real comfort, so for only 100 baht ($2) extra a night, it's smart to opt for comfort if you can.

Chiang Mai is getting more and more popular with tourists so prices are steadily going up and staying here for $20 a week is not really possible any longer. During busy times of the year you will also find that places fill up quickly, so make sure to book in advance if you have somewhere in particular that you want to stay.

Chiang Mai isn't an enormous city but with accommodation so cheap it is slightly foolish to save 100 baht a night to stay cheaper in the outskirts. A ride into the old city or near the riverside could easily cost you twice that if you are not careful.

Staying in the old city is the most popular choice with tourists for obvious reasons. It's the heart of the city's attractions and places of interest. The most popular areas are around Phae Gate and just east of the city walls. If you plan to spend the night going to bars or eating out late you might want to stay closer to the riverside or around the Night Bazaar.

It will be noisier around the bazaar, but you will often only be a 10 to 20-minute walk from the big tourist attractions and you won't have to walk too far late at night.

If you are interested in staying for cheap or for longer term, you might consider going northwest towards the large student community. It doesn't have as much choice in terms of hotels and guesthouses, but there are many short term flats that go for as little as 4,000 baht a month or about 150 baht a day.

BUDGET ACCOMMODATION

FWD House Hostel

This is a very charming and clean hostel that still offers excellent value at only 180 baht per person, per night. It is located in the old city and is in perfect walking distance of restaurants, temples, and bars.

Julie Guest House

This is a fantastic little guest house located east of the old city. It offers all the essentials including wi-fi, as well as relatively good food and lots of services for guests to help you out on your travels. Rooms come to 180 baht per person.

Thapae Gate Lodge

You can probably guess that this guesthouse is located very conveniently in the old city. It's a very solid, clean, and pleasant place to stay with air conditioning and extra amenities if you want to pay up for them. An average room is 200 baht a night.

MID RANGE ACCOMMODATION

Ping River Inn

This is a fairly simple lodging, but it is conveniently located by the riverside and night markets, and it has everything you need from a good place to stay. It's clean and easy going. For 500 baht a night the price isn't too bad either.

S.K. House II

Another solid choice for reasonably priced accommodation that is clean, spacious, and comes with everything you need including a rooftop lounge. Rooms come to 400 baht a night.

Royal Guest House

This is a larger guest house that caters to several different price ranges and offers good views of the city and comfortable accommodation. It is located just south of Phae Gate, and prices vary from 200 baht to 700.

HIGH END ACCOMMODATION

Mo Rooms

A really unique and superbly designed hotel with each room boasting its own theme and design features. If you want your accommodations to be as interesting as the city, this is the place to come. Mo Rooms is located just outside the old city, and comes with all the modern conveniences including swimming pool, travel agency and in-room fridges. At 2,800 baht a night you will be paying more for it though.

Tamarind Village

Located within the old city walls this is one of the most intriguing and character-filled hotels in the area. Rooms are tastefully and luxuriously fitted out, and it comes with its own full restaurant, spa, and swimming pool. If you want style and elegance during your stay you can't do much better than Tamarind Village. Rooms cost 5,000 baht a night but you're unlikely to regret it.

EATING OUT

The food in Chiang Mai is one of its most exciting elements and there is lots of choice whether you want typical Thai noodles, soups and curries, or you are hankering for Chinese or Western style food there are plenty of good choices that can compete for your money.

When it comes to Thai food there is the usual mix of phad Thai, sweet and sour Thai soup known as tom yam, comforting fried rice dishes known as Khao phat, or the delicious grilled chicken and sticky rice dish kai yang.

Chiang Mai is the place to come to try out authentic northern Thai cuisine. The most famous is Khao Soi which is a dish of yellow noodles in a cream coconut curry and serviced with deep fried noodles and vegetables. Kaeb Moo is a type of pork rind that is seasoned and deep fried and serviced with pandanus leaf: the original snack food. Hang ley is another local favorite and is a tasty and filling pork curry.

A lot of the best food will come from roadside stalls which can be found in the various markets around the city, the Kalare Food Centre near the Night Bazaar or the stalls along Intawarorot Road near the Three Kings Monument are some of the best places to check out. Pick somewhere that looks clean, that has locals lining up to eat, and hopefully has a menu you can point to.

Chiang Mai has a range of places to eat from coffee joints, cafes, restaurants, to buffets and fast food. Here are some of the best to look out for.

Khao Soi Khun Yai

You will see this place recommended a lot and for good reason. If you want to try northern Thai cuisine at its best this is the place to come. It has been a family run operation for several decades and locals, food snobs, and tourists alike keep coming back. Order the khao soi at least once.

Huen Phen

This is another fantastic place to come and try Northern Thai cuisine and you can try all the regional favorites and more, done right. There are no compromises here; it is a place serving food for locals, which is loved by tourists.

Bamboo Bee

This is a vegetarian restaurant in the old city that will show off what Thai cuisine can be, even without meat. You can also come here for a great range of lunch, breakfast, and even sweet treats.

Galae Garden Restaurant

This restaurant is a little pricier than many of the other alternatives on the street, but if you are looking for fresh and delicious grilled food this is the best place to come in possibly the whole city.

Angel's Secrets

This is a very popular café that serves wonderful snacks, breakfasts and delicious noodle dishes: you can try Tom Yam at its best here. Whether you are looking to get your energy back up with a pastry or to have some lunch, if you're in the east of the old city this is a great choice.

CONCLUSION

Chiang Mai is the gem of north of Thailand. It has beauty, brains and intrigues enough to delight any traveler lucky enough to pass through, and often it turns those travelers into residents.

Chiang Mai is a modern city with a lot to offer beyond its awe-inspiring scenery and temples: don't be afraid to live like a local and discover modern Thailand and all it can show you.

There is more to Chiang Mai than what this guide can give you, things which can only be offered on the massage table, in the temple grounds, or when trekking through the ancient hill tribes of Northern Thailand.

If you let it, Chiang Mai can be an experience you take with you everywhere you go and will allow you to take on a new spiritual and personal dimension. Don't be afraid to let yourself become part of the beautiful world that Chiang Mai has to offer.

Good luck with your journey and remember to stay relaxed the Chiang Mai way.

Made in the USA
Middletown, DE
26 January 2019